I love the still photograph.

A still picture can make people stop:
stop and look,
stop and read,
stop and think,
stop and dream,
stop and hope,
stop and shop,
stop and change,
stop turning the page.

A still picture is not a space filler;
it can be a powerful and concentrated moment of
thought, reflection, enjoyment, learning or remembering a moment.

Steve Coleman

For Mum and Dad

The Elmbridge Hundred

A Visual Journey

First published in Great Britain in 2014
by Asynjur Publishing
www.asynjur-publishing.com

Copyright © Astrid McGechan 2014
Competition entries copyright © each named photographer

Designed by Astrid McGechan
www.astridmcgechan.com

Jacket designed by Amy Blake (Brooklands College) and Astrid McGechan
www.brooklands.ac.uk

Based on an original idea: 'The Elmbridge Hundred' by Alistair Grant
Details of 'The Hundred' as listed on www.elmbridgehundred.org.uk

Printed and bound in Italy by Printer Trento S.r.l.
www.printertrento.com

ISBN 978-0-9929491-0-5

A CIP catalogue record for this book is available from the British Library.

The Elmbridge Hundred

A Visual Journey

Astrid McGechan

ASYNJUR
PUBLISHING

Sponsor

MUNDAYS.

Mundays LLP are delighted to sponsor *The Elmbridge Hundred – A Visual Journey*.

We are solicitors in the heart of Elmbridge and have been working with people and businesses in the borough for over five decades. We are proud of our heritage and strive to provide a truly outstanding service in a straightforward and approachable manner. To find out more about us visit www.mundays.co.uk.

It has been a privilege to sponsor this local project, which has brought together so many from the local community. Astrid McGechan and the student photographers have captured the beauty of Elmbridge in their stunning selection of photography. Congratulations to them all.

Valerie Toon

Managing Partner of Mundays LLP

Supporters

www.lightandland.co.uk   www.landscapesbywomen.co.uk

Contents

Introduction

When I first thought of creating a book about Elmbridge, I had my doubts. What would I photograph? Would I be able to find one hundred images? There are no spectacular mountain ranges, no picturesque waterfalls, no coastline.

But I soon realised that Elmbridge has much to offer. It lies in England's most wooded county – Surrey. Its woodland areas are of scientific importance. The Rivers Thames, Mole, Wey and Ember as well as several smaller streams cross its terrain, numerous historic landmarks grace its towns and villages, some of the finest English landscape gardens can be found in the borough, and it has a thriving and varied wildlife.

This book is a companion piece to 'The Elmbridge Hundred', a community project, which was set up in 2009 and brought together schools, museums, resident societies and charities in the quest to learn about and publicise the history and heritage of Elmbridge and to preserve it for future generations. From a shortlist of over six hundred notable people a panel selected those they considered the one hundred most influential residents who had lived in the borough. Those 'Hundred' are listed here in the places they are associated with; you can find their biographies on the project's website at www.elmbridgehundred.org.uk.

I need not have worried about whether I could muster the required number of photos. In fact, one hundred turned out to be far from enough to portray all the places and visual delights the borough has to offer. The selection presented here is only a small proportion of what caught my eye.

Elmbridge history is rich in famous individuals, who, sadly, are no longer here to be photographed. I have included instead some portraits of interesting present-day Elmbridge folk, people who make life in the borough tick.

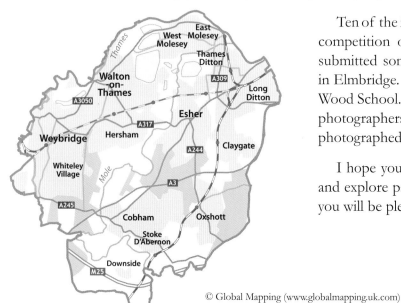

Ten of the images in this book are the winning entries of a photographic competition open to students from Elmbridge's senior schools. They submitted some wonderful work illustrating the variety of life and land in Elmbridge. The overall winner was Bryony Ross, a student at Hinchley Wood School. Her image, chosen by one of the UK's foremost landscape photographers, Charlie Waite, shows an interesting perspective of a pylon, photographed on Esher Common.

I hope you enjoy this book and will perhaps feel inspired to step out and explore parts of your borough that you don't yet know. I am certain you will be pleasantly surprised!

Astrid McGechan

© Global Mapping (www.globalmapping.uk.com)
Contains Ordnance Survey data © Crown copyright and database right 2013

Michael Aspel OBE

'The Elmbridge Hundred' is one of the most interesting projects I have been involved in. The project started in 2009 with the idea to select one hundred of the most influential residents in the borough's history; and those of us on the final selection panel had some lively and at times agonising sessions compiling that list.

Now, landscape photographer Astrid McGechan has produced a stunning companion piece – a visual journey, as she puts it, to complement the original project. As well as reaffirming the fascinating story of the borough, it will remind those of us lucky enough to live in Elmbridge that it is also a beautiful area.

Congratulations to Astrid and to all the young photographers she has persuaded to contribute to this captivating book.

Michael Aspel OBE
Honorary Freeman of the Borough of Elmbridge

Brooklands

As the birthplace of British motor sport and aviation and the home of many twentieth-century technologies, Brooklands is unrivalled. The motor course, constructed in 1907, was a wonder of its age. Much of the track and many of its original buildings and features have survived to this day, some as listed buildings or as part of a scheduled monument.

Built at Weybridge by the wealthy landowner Hugh Locke King in 1907 as a motor-racing circuit, Brooklands very soon became much more than that. For the next eighty years it was to remain a world-renowned centre of technological and engineering excellence. The racing circuit saw its heyday in the 1920s and 30s, when records were being set and broken by Malcolm Campbell, John Cobb and others in such magnificently crafted machines as Napier, Delage, Mercedes, Bentley and Bugatti, which were lovingly maintained by the finest mechanics in the land. Motorcycles and bicycles too had their devotees, and many records were established on the track. Brooklands was then a very fashionable place to be seen, becoming known as the 'Ascot of Motorsport'.

It was at Brooklands that A.V. Roe made pioneering powered flight trials with his first full-size aeroplane in 1908; here that Tommy Sopwith developed and flew the Sopwith Pup and Camel; and here too that the Hawker Hurricane and Vickers Wellington were built before and during the Second World War. The post-war years were distinguished by the achievements of the Vickers (later BAC and finally British Aerospace) factory, which produced a successful family of civil and military aircraft including the Viscount and VC10 airliners and contributed significantly to the design and manufacture of Concorde.

Although the outbreak of war in 1939 saw the end of racing on the legendary circuit, Brooklands maintained its position as the home of pioneering aviation development until British Aerospace ended aircraft production there in 1987. The Brooklands Museum Trust was formed that same year and continues to preserve the spirit and traditions of this unique heritage location today. [1]

[1] Based on www.brooklandsmuseum.com/index.php?/history (accessed January 2014) by kind permission of Brooklands Museum

Malcolm Campbell	(1885–1948)	racing driver
John Rhodes Cobb	(1899–1952)	racing driver
George Robert Edwards	(1908–2003)	aeronautical engineer
Hilda Beatrice Hewlett	(1864–1943)	aviator, aircraft designer, flying instructor
Hugh Fortescue Locke King	(1848–1926)	entrepreneur, motor-racing promoter
& Dame Ethel Locke King	(1864–1956)	motor-racing promoter, hospital patron
John Godfrey Parry Thomas	(1884–1927)	racing driver
Anthony Reid Railton	(1895–1977)	automobile engineer
Thomas Octave Murdoch Sopwith	(1888–1989)	aeronautical engineer
Barnes Neville Wallis	(1887–1979)	aeronautical engineer, designer
Paul Wyand	(1907–1968)	automobile engineer, film-maker

A Brooklands volunteer

Ralph Brough
Napier-Railton team member, Brooklands Museum

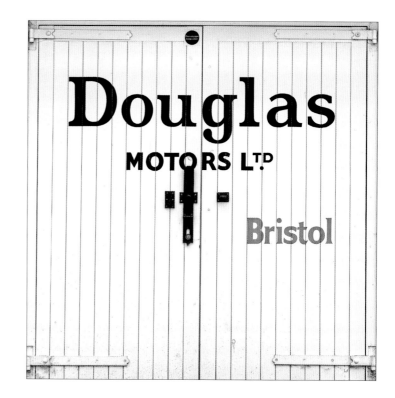

Doors of racing lockups, Brooklands Museum

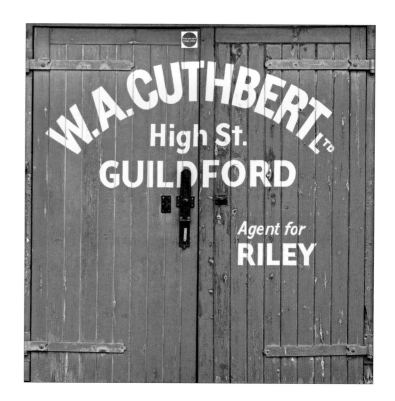

Concorde, Brooklands Museum

Concorde, Brooklands Museum

Lamp, 1935 Morris 10-6 Cunard Special, Austin Morris Day, Brooklands Museum

Badges, Austin Morris Day, Brooklands Museum

Engine of a Brough Superior motorbike, Brooklands Museum

Brooklands Community Park

Brooklands Community Park, covering an area of 60 acres, is on the site of the historic Brooklands motor racing circuit. Landscaped areas, open parkland and woodland provide ample scope for leisure activities. Grassland as well as established and newly planted vegetation support nature conservation efforts.

The park features walks and cycle paths along the River Wey and along sections of the former racetrack and aerodrome runway, as well as play areas, a skateboard park, a BMX track and a multi-court play area for football and basketball.

Wet leaves

Tree trunk

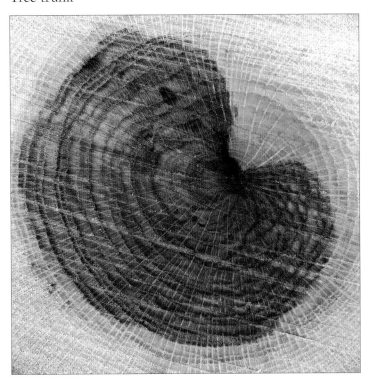

Ivy leaf

Claygate

Claygate is the only civil parish in Elmbridge. It is listed in the Domesday Book as a manor of Thames Ditton under the name of 'Claigate' and was held by Westminster Abbey until the sixteenth century, when it was added to Hampton Court after the Dissolution of the Monasteries. It grew and prospered in the mid-nineteenth century with the rise of the Claremont estate nearby, which attracted some wealthy and noble families to the village, and with the arrival of the railway in 1885, which turned Claygate into a place that could conveniently be reached from London.

The name of the village stems from local clay pits, which form part of the London Clay beds. Much of the surrounding area was supplied with bricks from Claygate, including Hampton Court Palace. Some street names still carry the legacy of the past, such as Forge Drive, Kilnside and Fishersdene, named after the clay pond. Brick production continued until well into the twentieth century.

Reflections on a classic car, Claygate Flower and Village Show

 THE ELMBRIDGE HUNDRED   Frank Arthur Worsley   (1872–1943)   explorer, traveller

'Real people have real fires.'

David Russell, chimney sweep
Claygate

Cobham

Cobham appeared in the Domesday Book as 'Covenham', held by Chertsey Abbey. It lies on the River Mole and incorporates two historically distinct communities, which grew along the road to London (Street Cobham) and around St Andrew's Church (Church Cobham). Parts of St Andrew's, such as the tower and tower arch, date back to the twelfth century.

The proximity of Cobham to Brooklands racetrack and airfield resulted in the establishment of automotive manufacturers and the use of various related facilities by the aircraft manufacturer Vickers-Armstrong. From 1933 until 1940 the engineer Reid Railton produced Railton cars at the Fairmile works in Cobham. After an attack by the Luftwaffe in 1940, Vickers-Armstrong moved its experimental department to several secret locations on the nearby Silvermere and Foxwarren Park estates, where Barnes Wallis continued some of his trials while developing the 'bouncing bomb'. Silver Hawk Motors (1920–21), Invicta Car (1925–33) and Huron (1970s) produced sports and racing cars in Cobham.

Grist Mill

The history of water mills along the Mole in Cobham dates back to the Middle Ages. The last to be constructed remains one of Cobham's landmarks today. It was built in 1822 and operated until 1928. A large part of the mill was demolished in 1953 to accommodate a widened Mill Road. Only the grist mill remains, which was restored to working order in 1993 and is looked after by the Cobham Mill Preservation Trust.

Harvey Christian Combe	(1752–1818)	brewer, businessman
William Hoste	(1780–1828)	Royal Navy captain
John Ligonier	(1680–1770)	Commander in Chief of the British Army
David Lloyd George	(1863–1945)	prime minister
Vernon Lushington	(1832–1912)	lawyer
Humphrey Lynde	(1579–1636)	politician
Albert Noel Campbell Macklin	(1886–1946)	automobile engineer
Robert McAlpine	(1847–1934)	civil engineer
& Thomas Malcolm McAlpine	(1877–1967)	civil engineer, son of Robert McAlpine
John Roddam Spencer Stanhope	(1829–1908)	painter

THE ELMBRIDGE HUNDRED

Cobham Community Tile Project display

Rooted, Fairmile Common

Tree and sky, Plough Lane

'Hip to Hip' trick, skate park Cobham, photographed by Daniel Leach-Walton, Rydens Enterprise School and Sixth Form College

Barn door, Downside Road

Hatchford Mausoleum

Fence, Downside Road

Fungus, Chatley Heath

Fern, Chatley Heath

Painshill

Painshill is one of the finest eighteenth-century English landscape gardens.

The 1730s saw the Landscape Movement beginning to influence garden designs in England. Inspired by Dutch paintings of the sixteenth and seventeenth centuries, the movement promoted the integration of artistic, philosophical and scientific ideas from all over the world into the design of English landscape gardens. Geometric lines and forms were replaced by curves and natural shapes, and the formality of previous garden designs gave way to a more organic style. The garden at Painshill was one of the earliest to reflect this change in fashion.

After extensive tours in Italy, in 1738 the Hon. Charles Hamilton MP acquired land at Painshill with the aim of creating 'living paintings' in a new type of garden. He spent thirty-five years developing his garden before financial constraints forced him in 1773 to sell the estate. Hamilton combined newly introduced and rare plant species with classical buildings and other features, such as the Ruined Abbey, the Mausoleum, the Crystal Grotto, the Temple of Bacchus, the Turkish Tent and the Gothic Tower. Central to the garden is the Serpentine Lake, which, together with its surroundings, now provides a valuable habitat for birds and bats. The landscape presents various styles, including formal ornamental settings around the Amphitheatre, the Alpine Valley featuring a meadow and mature woodland and the Elysian Plains with its scattering of trees, flowering shrubs and flowerbeds. From the Bastion on top of Wood Hill visitors can enjoy one of the finest 'living paintings' that Hamilton created. The view includes the vineyard and Serpentine Lake and extends all the way to the North Downs.

Theatre of plants, Small Walled Garden

| Matthew Arnold | (1822–1888) | poet, writer, educationalist |
| Charles Hamilton | (1704–1786) | garden designer, naturalist |

'Working to preserve Mr Hamilton's Painshill so that current and future generations can enjoy one of the finest English landscape gardens.'

Mark Ebdon, estate manager
Painshill Park Trust

Branching out

Chinese Bridge

Bluebells

Waterwheel

Mausoleum

View towards the Gothic Temple

East and West Molesey

A reference to 'Muleseg' ('Mul's Island') can be found as far back as the seventh century, possibly suggesting that Molesey does not get its name from the River Mole, which – together with the River Ember – flows through this suburban village. The Domesday Book mentions 'Molesham', and the division between East and West Molesey first appeared in the twelfth century. The border between the two Moleseys is marked by the Molesey Stone, just outside the Walton Road library.

Henry VIII's Hampton Court Palace, constructed in the early 1500s by Cardinal Wolsey, and later the arrival of the railway in 1849, contributed to the growth and development of Molesey. The first bridge across the Thames there was built in 1753.

Molesey Riverside with Hampton Court Bridge

THE ELMBRIDGE HUNDRED

Terence Tenison Cuneo   (1907–1996)   artist
Henry Thompson   (1820–1904)   physician, writer

'What I did yesterday, I can do today. What I do today, I can do tomorrow. This is the motto that takes me through life.'

June Bland, actress
Artistic Director of the Barn Theatre Club, founder of the Old School

Sailing on the River Thames

Autumn colours, Emberside Recreation Ground

Hurst Park

Hurst Park sits at the northeast tip of Elmbridge, by the River Thames, just upstream from Hampton Court Bridge. It covers an area of roughly 80 acres and incorporates Hurst Meadows and Little Hurst Meadows. The park was created and has been maintained over the past twenty-five years by Elmbridge Borough Council.

It was previously known as Molesey Hurst, which was first mentioned in 1249 with a transfer of meadowland belonging to the Manor of Molesey Matham. The meadow was used as 'Lammas land', which permitted the grazing of cattle from Lammas Day (1 August) until Candlemas (2 February).[2]

The park's use for leisure activities dates back several centuries. Boxing, duelling, golf, cricket, cock-fighting, archery, prize fighting, ballooning, pony racing and more had been popular since the seventeenth century, but petered out when a race course was established there in 1890. The races were at one time as popular as those held at Kempton and Sandown Park, but the course closed in 1962 and access for the public was restored. The park featured a bathing station, which opened in 1925 but closed in 1966 after a fire. Established in 1867, Molesey Regatta takes place on the river each July.

Sunrise

Hurst Meadows are a rare meadowland habitat created by Elmbridge Borough Council through tree planting and the seeding of wild grasses and flowers.

The meadows come to life each spring with an abundance of bees, butterflies, moths and other insects as well as thriving bird populations. After sunset, bats can often be seen foraging. Pathways criss-cross the meadows and invite visitors from near and far to explore and enjoy their beauty.

[2] Rowland G. M. Baker, *Thameside Molesey*. Barracuda Books, 1989, as cited by Friends of Hurst Park, www.friendsofhurstpark.org.uk (accessed October 2013)

THE ELMBRIDGE HUNDRED   William [Silver Billy] Beldham   (1766–1862)   cricketer

Boat moored on the Thames

Snow

Riverside

Light and shadow

Molesey Heath

Molesey Heath, covering 42 acres, does not constitute heathland in the traditional sense. Initially a gravel pit, it was later used as a landfill site.

Since activities ceased, rough grassland and shrubs have taken over. This in turn has provided for a rich wildlife. Insects such as burrowing bees and a variety of birds, including redshanks and little ringed plovers, can be observed.

Coppiced willow

Tree bark

Hawthorn berries

Esher

Esher, on the River Mole, was first mentioned in the Domesday Book as 'Aissela'. In the sixteenth century, Henry VIII made the countryside around Esher, close to his residence at Hampton Court, into a hunting ground. The eighteenth century saw the construction and extension of Claremont Garden and mansion, initially by the playwright and architect John Vanbrugh and Thomas Pelham-Holles, Duke of Newcastle, and later under the ownership of Robert Clive of India. For a long time, Esher was one of the main stagecoach stops along the London to Portsmouth road.

The impressive Grade II listed Esher Place has seen a turbulent history. Peter des Roches, Bishop of Winchester, bought the site in the thirteenth century; in the late fifteenth, William Waynflete, Bishop of Winchester and Lord Chancellor, owned it. He rebuilt the house and added a tower gatehouse – Waynflete's Tower. Via Cardinal Wolsey, Henry VIII, Elizabeth I and Lord Howard of Effingham the estate was passed to the Drake family. The years between 1634 and 1716 witnessed at least another seven owners before the estate was split from the mansion and sold to the Duke of Newcastle. In 1729, then owned by the Duke's younger brother Henry Pelham, the house was torn down again and rebuilt. Just the gatehouse was left untouched. In 1805 one John Spicer, a merchant, bought the house, only to demolish it again and erect yet another, this one in a more elevated position. Edgar Vincent, later 1st Lord d'Abernon, purchased the house and remaining grounds in 1895. In 1930 the latter were sold for development and he passed the house to the Ragged School Union. A children's home until 1952, it was eventually bought by the Electrical Trades Union (now Unite the Union) and turned into a college. Grade I listed Waynflete's Tower, in private ownership, still stands today.

Frederick James Archer	(1857–1886)	jockey
Dudley Carleton	(1574–1632)	politician
Frances Day	(1908–1984)	actress, singer
William Dockwra	(1635–1716)	businessman, copper and brass manufacturer
Alban Patrick Gwynne	(1913–2003)	architect
Walter Reginald Hammond	(1903–1965)	cricketer
George Harrison	(1943–2001)	musician, film producer
William Howitt	(1792–1879)	writer, father of Alfred and Anna
& Alfred William Howitt	(1830–1908)	anthropologist
& Anna Mary Howitt	(1824–1884)	painter, illustrator, author, feminist activist
Augusta Ada Lovelace	(1815–1852)	computer scientist
Arthur Onslow	(1691–1768)	politician
Henry Pelham	(1694–1754)	prime minister
Robert Cedric Sherriff	(1896–1975)	playwright
William Wayneflete	(1395–1486)	government official, philanthropist
Francis John Williamson	(1833–1920)	artist
Thomas Wolsey	(1471–1530)	Archbishop of York, statesman

The Elmbridge Hundred

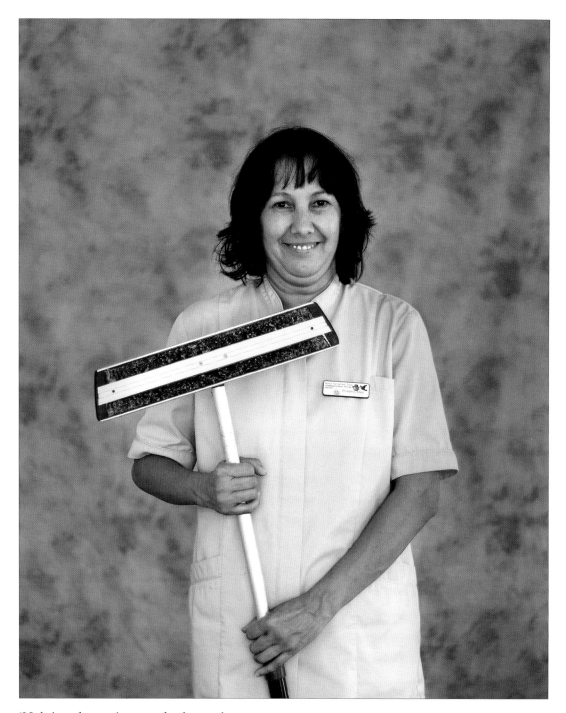

'Helping the patients to be happy.'

Maria Fernandez Sosa, housekeeping/ward-services assistant
Princess Alice Hospice, Esher

St George's Church was built around 1540 and is Esher's oldest public building. It was the town's parish church for three-hundred years, but by the mid-nineteenth century it could no longer accommodate the growing congregation and was replaced by Christ Church. This means that St George's has remained largely untouched and retains many of its Tudor features. The seventeenth century clock mechanism is still housed in the wooden clock turret. The 'Newcastle-Pew', with its own entrance, was designed by Vanbrugh and added in 1725–26 for the Duke of Newcastle. The pew was later divided into several compartments, one of which Esher Place residents were granted the privilege of using.

St George's is now cared for by the Churches Conservation Trust.

In memoriam..., St George's Church

Vine, West End Lane

Claremont Landscape Garden

Initially bought and built on by Sir John Vanbrugh in 1709, Chargate Farm became Claremont in 1714 when Thomas Pelham-Holles, Earl of Clare and later Duke of Newcastle, bought the estate. The house was later extended. In 1769 the estate passed to Robert Clive of India, who commissioned Lancelot 'Capability' Brown to replace the house with a larger mansion. From the early 1800s until 1922 Claremont was used as a royal residence, first by Charlotte, Princess of Wales, and her husband Leopold, Prince of Saxe-Coburg-Saalfeld, and later by Queen Victoria, the former French king Louis-Philippe and Prince Leopold, Duke of Albany. In 1922 the estate was broken up and a large part of it sold for development. Most of the secondary buildings were demolished. In 1930 the mansion became part of what is now known as Claremont Fan Court School.

Doves

THE ELMBRIDGE HUNDRED

Charlotte Augusta	(1796–1817)	Princess of Wales
Robert Clive of India	(1725–1774)	government official, military leader
William Duckitt the elder	(unknown)	agriculturalist, inventor
Leopold I.	(1790–1865)	King of Belgium
Louis Philippe	(1773–1850)	exiled King of France
& Marie-Amélie Thérèse	(1782–1866)	exiled Queen, wife of Louis Philippe
Thomas Pelham-Holles	(1693–1768)	statesman
& Harriet Pelham-Holles	(1707–1776)	socialite, wife of Thomas Pelham-Holles
Robert Taylor Pritchett	(1828–1907)	artist, gun maker
John Vanbrugh	(1664–1726)	architect, playwright
Queen Victoria	(1819–1901)	monarch

Bench and amphitheatre, Claremont Landscape Garden, photographed by Pierro Pozella, Hinchley Wood School

Grotto

Claremont is one of the earliest examples of the eighteenth-century English landscape garden. At one time it covered an area of 1,500 acres and featured a pleasure ground, a flower garden, ponds, woods, a farm, a deer park and a kitchen garden that grew fruit and vegetables for the occupants of the house. The surviving 49 acres of the garden have retained their original layout to this day. Visitors can explore the turf Amphitheatre, the Serpentine Lake and its Grotto, the Camellia Terrace and the Thatched Cottage. The Belvedere Tower, now owned by Claremont Fan Court School, opens to the public on certain days.

Belvedere Tower

Esher Commons

There are several woodland areas that are collectively known as the Esher Commons. Situated at the northern end of Surrey and southwest of Esher, they comprise Esher Common, West End Common, Arbrook Common, Fairmile Common and Oxshott Heath. Combined, the commons cover 890 acres (four per cent of the Borough of Elmbridge). Apart from the extensive deciduous and coniferous woodlands, visitors can enjoy grassland, marshes, bogs and ponds. This diversity sustains many habitats, which support an amazing variety of plant species and animals. Perhaps their greatest claim to fame is the abundant fungi: more than 3,100 species have been counted, making the commons one of the areas with the largest numbers of fungi recorded in places of similar size in the world! Lizards and grass snakes also find an excellent home in the commons, especially on Oxshott Heath, where the hilly slopes face south.

Woodland path, Esher Common

The woodland areas of Arbrook Common are home to many species of songbird as well as kestrels, sparrowhawks and tawny owls. West End Common includes The Ledges, a stretch of mature and partly ancient trees on a bank of high ground running alongside the River Mole. The ponds of West End Common, which support many species of dragonfly and damselfly as well as water scorpions, diving beetles and freshwater shrimps, are regularly managed, which protects their 'star resident', the rare *Damasonium alisma*, or starfruit by its common name. In 2005 Chequers Pond was the only site in the UK where flowering starfruit were recorded.

The Esher Commons were designated a Site of Special Scientific Interest (SSSI) in 1955 by what was then the Nature Conservancy (now English Nature).

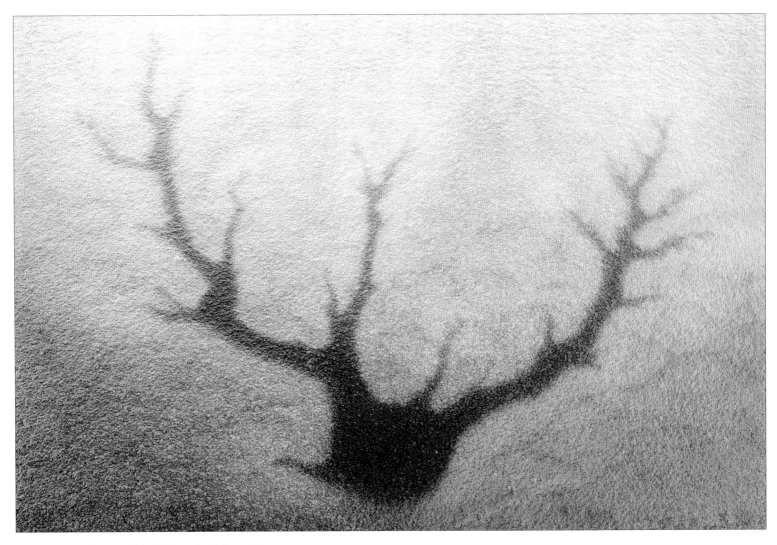

Patterns on frozen Black Pond, Esher Common

Path, Arbrook Common

Beech trees, The Ledges

Swan, Black Pond, Esher Common, photographed by Havana Coleman-Wood, Esher Church of England High School

Little Red Riding Hood loses her hood and basket, woodland near West End Lane, photographed by Jack Milburn, Rydens Enterprise School and Sixth Form College

Path and trees, Esher Common, photographed by
Emilie Heatley, Esher Church of England High School

Black Pond, Esher Common, photographed by Jade McLagan,
Esher Church of England High School

Pylon, Esher Common, photographed by Bryony Ross, Hinchley Wood School, competition winner

Hinchley Wood

Hinchley Wood is a mainly residential suburban village. The farmland it was built on was previously part of Thames Ditton but the community grew substantially with the opening of the railway station in 1930. Hinchley Wood's first church, St Christopher's, was built in 1953.

The village is close to Littleworth Common. To the southwest, one of the most popular walking spots is Telegraph Hill, which features a Grade II listed semaphore tower.

Fungi, Telegraph Hill, Hinchley Wood, photographed by Pierro Pozella, Hinchley Wood School

Fox, Hinchley Wood Station, photographed by Pierro Pozella, Hinchley Wood School

Hersham

Hersham is a village by the River Mole, just south of Walton-on-Thames. Flint instruments dating back to the Mesolithic period have been found near the river, indicating the presence of a prehistoric settlement. Later, Anglo-Saxons settled in the district and gave Hersham its name, often spelled 'Haverichesham' in medieval times.

Several films and TV programmes, such as *Monty Python's Flying Circus*, *Nighty Night* and a series of the crime drama *Ashes to Ashes*, have been filmed in Hersham, thanks to its proximity to Shepperton and London studios.

Visitors can enjoy walks along the river in Hersham Riverside Park or explore nearby Esher Commons.

Plane leaves, Molesey Road

Colours, seen at Carter's Steam Fair

PURPLE YELLOW RED
ORANGE RED PURPLE
GREEN BLUE ORANGE

THE ELMBRIDGE HUNDRED

William Lilly	(1602–1681)	astrologer
Jane Margaret Scott	(1779–1839)	actress, musician, theatre manager
Hugh Montague Trenchard	(1873–1956)	Air Force officer
William Whiteley	(1831–1907)	businessman, philanthropist

'Teaching our children to cross safely!'

Julie McGee, lollipop lady
Bell Farm Primary School, Hersham

Oxshott

Listed as 'Occesete' in 1179, Oxshott formed part of Stoke d'Abernon for several centuries. Its name means 'Ocga's corner of land', from 'sceat' describing exactly the latter and 'Ocga' being an old English name. Until 1912 an alternative spelling of 'Ockshot' was commonly found. The arrival of the railway in 1885 changed Oxshott's character and the village expanded significantly. Its first church, St Andrew's, was consecrated in 1912 and Oxshott became a parish in 1913. During the Second World War Canadian troops were stationed on Oxshott Heath, which, together with the Prince's Covert, surrounds the village.

In the late nineteenth century the heath experienced significant vandalism, which concerned local folk so much that they demanded a public inquiry. In 1904 an Act of Parliament bestowed responsibility for the management of the heath on nine honorary conservators, an arrangement that is still in place today. Although owned by Elmbridge Borough Council, it is the local people who look after the heath, now designated a Site of Special Scientific Interest.

Breaking through, Oxshott Heath

Cones, Oxshott Heath

Robert George Collier Proctor   (1868–1903)   inventor, linguist, traveller, librarian

'Traditional butchery in modern times.'

Simon Taylor, butcher
Surrey Hill Butchers, Oxshott

Tree, Oxshott Heath

Grass, Oxshott Heath

Trees and sky, near Blundel Lane

Stoke d'Abernon

The Domesday Book already listed a church among the assets of 'Stoche', the Saxon place name for Stoke, which at the time described a palisaded farmstead. The addition of 'd'Abernon' derived from Sir Roger D'Aubernoun, who came to England during the Norman Conquest and was awarded land in return for his allegiance to William the Conqueror.

St Mary's Church, believed to be the oldest in Surrey, is of Saxon origin and was built in the late seventh or early eighth century as a 'proprietary' church – one built on private land by a feudal lord, who retained the right to appoint clergy. A substantial part of the Saxon church survives to this day.

St Mary's is famous for its medieval brasses dating back to the fourteenth century. The brass of Sir John d'Abernon the Elder is unusual in that it shows a knight with both a lance and a sword as well as featuring enamel on its shield. It is regarded as one of the finest military brasses in England.

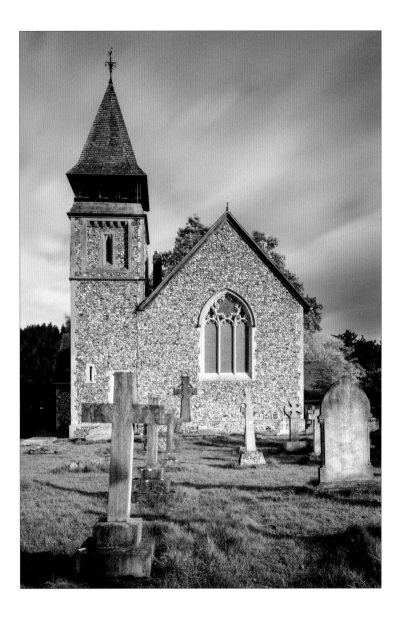

St Mary's Church

THE ELMBRIDGE HUNDRED			
Frederick Carkeet William Bryant	(1843–1888)	businessman
Yehudi Menuhin	(1916–1999)	violinist, conductor
Edgar Vincent	(1857–1941)	politician, diplomat, art collector
& Helen Venetia Vincent	(1866–1954)	linguist, nurse anaesthetist, wife of Edgar

'Plants help make people happy!'

David Phillips, landscape gardener
Seymours Landscapes

Thames Ditton

Originally a Saxon farmstead or settlement called Dictun, Ditton was listed in the Domesday Book comprising two parts – 'Ditone' and 'Ditune'. The riverside manor and parish formed Thames Ditton. Other places that at various times constituted parts of Thames Ditton were Weston (initially 'Westtun', or 'West Farm'), Imber Court (initially 'Limeurde', later 'Immewurth', meaning 'Imma's farm') and some Claygate lands. The Priory, originally a Georgian mansion, was said to be one of the finest buildings between Hampton and Windsor. First owned by Lord St Leonards and later by Charlotte Boyle Walsingham, its last use before closure was as a care home for the elderly, poor and needy, run by the Sisters of Compassion. Giggs Hill Green, a triangular park by Portsmouth Road, features the village's cricket pitch. The origins of its name remain unclear, as there is no hill in the vicinity.

Sweet chestnuts, Thames Ditton, photographed by Laura Harmer, Hinchley Wood School

THE ELMBRIDGE HUNDRED

Edward Fitzgerald	(1763–1798)	Irish nationalist, army officer
& Pamela Fitzgerald	(1773–1831)	political activist, wife of Edward
& Henry Fitzgerald	(1761–1829)	actor, brother of Edward
Fred Karno	(1866–1941)	businessman, comedian, theatre manager
George London	(d. 1714)	garden designer
Thomas Babington Macaulay	(1800–1859)	historian, poet, writer
Cesar Picton	(1754–1836)	businessman, traveller
Heathfield Harman Stephenson	(1833–1896)	cricketer
Peter William Willans	(1851–1892)	mechanical engineer

'People and books – what could be nicer!'

Gloria Hiscock, librarian
Dittons Library

Autumn colours, Giggs Hill

Bench, Giggs Hill

Walton-on-Thames

Well before the arrival of the Romans and Saxons, Celtic settlers populated this area. These people were described by the Anglo-Saxons as 'wealas', meaning 'foreigners'. In the Domesday Book Walton appears as 'Waletona'.

While the River Thames with its local crossing at Cowey Sale has played an important role in Walton's history, its bridges have inspired famous artists such as Canaletto, who painted the first Walton bridge shortly after it opened in 1750, and William Turner, who immortalised the second bridge, built in 1788, while on his sketching tour along the Thames and Wey in 1805.

Walton-on-Thames had its own film studios, which greatly contributed to British film-making for more than 60 years. Cecil Hepworth set up Hepworth Studios in 1899, but went bankrupt in 1923. Consequently over 2,000 films, representing almost 80 per cent of British output between 1900 and 1929, were sold off and lost; but luckily, many were later rescued.[3] In 1926 the studios were bought by Archibald Nettlefold and reopened as Nettlefold Studios. In the 1950s Sapphire Films took over the enterprise, now called Walton Studios, and produced TV series such as *The Adventures of Robin Hood*, *The Adventures of Sir Lancelot*, *The Buccaneers*, *Sword of Freedom* and *The Four Just Men*. The studios closed in 1961 and were demolished. Only the power-generating house, originally built by Hepworth and converted into a theatre in 1925, remains and is now known as the Walton Playhouse.

Window at the Swan Pub

[3] www.john-goodwin.com/hepworth/the_studios.htm (accessed March 2014)

THE ELMBRIDGE HUNDRED

Samuel Dicker	(d. 1760)	entrepreneur, politician
Richard D'Oyly Carte	(1844–1901)	theatre manager, father of Rupert
& Rupert D'Oyly Carte	(1876–1948)	theatre manager, father of Bridget Cicely
& Bridget Cicely D'Oyly Carte	(1908–1985)	theatre manager
William Henry Grenfell	(1855–1945)	athlete, politician
Cecil Milton Hepworth	(1874–1953)	film-maker
Louis Alexander Mountbatten	(1854–1921)	Royal Family member
& Victoria Alberta Mountbatten	(1863–1950)	Royal Family member, wife of Louis Alexander
Edward [Lumpy] Stevens	(1735–1819)	cricketer, gardener
Howard Overing Sturgis	(1855–1920)	novelist
& Julian Russell Sturgis	(1848–1904)	novelist, poet, amateur footballer
Arthur Seymour Sullivan	(1842–1900)	composer
Harriet Mill	(1807–1858)	philosopher, women's rights champion, writer
Alma Taylor	(1895–1974)	actress, co-star of the Tilly Girl series
& Chrissie White	(1895–1989)	actress, co-star of the Tilly Girl series
Alan Turing	(1912–1954)	computer scientist, mathematician
Hannah Weinstein	(1911–1984)	film-maker, journalist

'A friendly familiar face and reliable service are what a majority of people like.'

Gary Bennett, milkman
Dairy Crest, Walton-on-Thames and Weybridge

Swans, River Thames at Cowey Sale

Autumn leaves, Shaw Drive

Buttercups and daisies, Shaw Drive

Grey heron, Shaw Drive Pond

The weir, Sunbury Lock Ait

Spring blossom, Terrace Road

Weybridge

Weybridge gets its name from the River Wey, which straddles the town on its eastern side before flowing into the Thames close to Shepperton Lock. In the Domesday Book Weybridge appeared as Webruge, though its history stretches back to the Iron Age. Evidence of a hill fort has been found on top of St George's Hill.

For centuries just a small riverside village, it came to prominence in 1537 when Henry VIII took possession of a manor house owned by the Rede family and turned it into Oatlands Palace. Although he rarely visited, he was married there to his fifth wife Catherine Howard. The palace became a favourite of Queen Elizabeth I, who used it as a hunting lodge. Demolition of the palace started in 1649 after the execution of Charles I. Some of its bricks were later sold and found a new use as a lining for the Wey Navigation canal, which opened in 1653, making it one of the earliest canals in the country. Today the Oatlands Park Hotel stands on part of the old palace grounds.

Richard Cawston	(1923–1986)	film-maker
Henry Clinton	(1730–1795)	army officer
Harry Cohen	(1912–2000)	headmaster, religious figure, politician
Charlie Drake	(1925–2006)	comedian, actor, writer, singer
Martin Eric Dunbar-Nasmith	(1883–1965)	submariner, naval officer
John Easthope	(1784–1865)	entrepreneur, politician
Edward Morgan Forster	(1879–1970)	writer
Myles Birket Foster	(1825–1899)	illustrator, painter, engraver
Frederic Augustus	(1763–1827)	Royal Family member
& Frederica Charlotte	(1767–1820)	Royal Family member, wife of Frederic
Eric Gardner	(1877–1951)	historian, physician
Amy Constance Gentry	(1903–1976)	rower, secretary to Barnes Wallis
Henry VIII	(1491–1547)	monarch
James IV and I	(1566–1625)	monarch
Frances Anne Kemble	(1809–1893)	actress, writer, social reformer
John Lennon	(1940–1980)	musician, political activist
George Meredith	(1828–1909)	novelist, poet
Henry Fiennes Pelham-Clinton	(1720–1794)	Second Duke of Newcastle-under-Lyme
Home Riggs Popham	(1762–1820)	naval officer, inventor
Benjamin Scott	(1814–1892)	Chamberlain of the City of London
Walter George Tarrant	(1875–1942)	aeronautical engineer
John Tradescant the elder	(1570–1638)	collector, gardener, naturalist, traveller
Brian George Wenham	(1937–1997)	media consultant, broadcasting executive
Richard Weston	(1591–1652)	canal builder, agriculturalist
Gerrard Winstanley	(1609–1676)	religious reformer, Digger

'To serve and protect the community.'

PC Robert Betts, policeman
Neighbourhood specialist officer for Weybridge

Reflections, Wey Navigation

Thistle, Churchfields Meadow

Six-spot burnet moths, Churchfields Meadow

Weybridge Heath

Covering 47 acres, the heath is part of Weybridge Common. It stretches from the South Western Main Line railway to Cobbetts Hill.

In the past the heath was home to several rare types of insects, birds and insectivorous plants. Its ants were of particular interest to the British entomologist Horace Donisthorpe, who gained many of his insights from studying their colonies.

Having been left to its own devices for many years, the heath now resembles young woodland, but attempts have recently been made to reverse the process and re-establish the lost heathland habitat.

Tree on Weybridge Heath

Impressions from the annual fireworks display at Cleves School, Oatlands

Bibliography

Diane Cooper, 'Explore Surrey's Countryside'. www.surreycc.gov.uk/?a=199921, (accessed January 2013)

John Morris, *Domesday Book Surrey*, Phillimore 1975

Elmbridge Borough Council, 'Brooklands Community Park in Elmbridge', www.elmbridge.gov.uk/leisure/parks/brooklands.htm (accessed February 2014)

Claygate Parish Council, 'The Story of Claygate', claygate.info/-history-of-claygate.html (accessed December 2013)

David Taylor, *Cobham: A History*, Phillimore 2008

Sally Rowat, *Painshill Reborn*, Painshill Park Trust 2010

Michael Symes, *Mr Hamilton's Elysium: The Gardens of Painshill*, Frances Lincoln 2010

http://en.wikipedia.org/wiki/Molesey (accessed October 2013)

www.friendsofhurstpark.org.uk (accessed October 2013)

Felix Palmer, 'Old Esher Place', as cited by Esher Place, www.esherplace.com/home/a-history-of-esher-place (accessed October 2013)

www.stgeorgesesher.org/history.htm (accessed October 2013)

Claremont Landscape Garden, The National Trust 2012

Laura Mayer, *Capability Brown and the English Landscape Garden*, Shire Publications 2011

Roger Turner, *Capability Brown and the Eighteenth Century English Landscape*, Phillimore 1999

History of the Esher Commons; Exploring the Esher Commons; Exploring the Elmbridge Countryside, Elmbridge Borough Council 2007

George Greenwood, *Hersham in Surrey: A brief local history of the parish of St Peter's, Hersham, in the Borough of Elmbridge in Surrey*, 1986

en.wikipedia.org/wiki/hersham (accessed March 2014)

B. S. Gidvani, *Oxshott: The Story of a Surrey Village,* Baron 1996

www.oxshottheath.org/history (accessed May 2014)

St Mary's Church Stoke d'Abernon, 'History', www.stmarysstokedabernon.co.uk (accessed October 2013)

Philip J. Burchett, *A Historical Sketch of Thames Ditton*, Basing Press 1985

en.wikipedia.org/wiki/thames_ditton (accessed April 2014)

Michael E. Blackman, *A Short History of Walton-on-Thames*, Walton & Weybridge Local History Society 1989

en.wikipedia.org/wiki/walton-on-thames (accessed March 2014)

www.weybridgesociety.org.uk/Oatlands_Palace_History (accessed May 2014)

www.weybridgesociety.org.uk/History_of_Weybridge (accessed May 2014)

Acknowledgements

I am deeply grateful to Charlie Waite for his ideas, inspiration, encouragement and support.

I'd like to thank Hamish and Paula for their enthusiasm and patience over the last three years, which gave me the time and space to work on my book.

My appreciation goes to all who contributed their time, knowledge and passion, especially:

Michael Aspel OBE
Ed Stewart
Elmbridge Hundred Steering Committee (www.elmbridgehundred.org.uk)
Jackie Freshfield (www.jackiefreshfield.com)
Victoria Allen (Brooklands College)
Brooklands College (www.brooklands.ac.uk)
Michal Porecki
Sue Phillpott
Steve Coleman (www.lightinframe.com)

I also thank Brooklands Museum, Painshill Park Trust Limited and the National Trust for allowing me to photograph at Brooklands Museum, Painshill and Claremont Landscape Garden for this book.

Most of the images from this book are available as signed archival prints. Please visit www.astridmcgechan.com for details.